The Myrrh-Bearers

The Myrrh-Bearers

Judith Crispin

PUNCHER & WATTMANN

First published in 2015

Published by Puncher and Wattmann
PO Box 441
Glebe NSW 2037

http://www.puncherandwattmann.com
puncherandwattmann@bigpond.com

National Library of Australia
Cataloguing-in-Publication entry:

Crispin, Judith

The Myrrh-Bearers

ISBN   9781922186782

I. Title.

A821.3

Cover design by Matthew Holt

Printed by McPherson's Printing Group

This project has been assisted by the Australian Government through the Australia Council, its arts funding and advisory body.

Australian Government

Australia Council
for the Arts

Contents

I. He is a machine, a predictability.
Sometimes his body is inhabited by bulls or red hares.

La Porte Étroite

—for Emmanuel Nunes

He remembered the inside of her womb—starry
as a church lit by pleroma
or some interior sun;
remembered looking out from the comet's tail
into space sewn with rays,
her red walls pinpricked by lights,
at a distance impossible to gauge,
like the height of sky where no difference exists
between aeroplanes and stars.

And blue were those first nights
in which he woke vertiginous,
the void opening beneath his bed,
a void he wished to see,
but pushed fists into his eyes to stop seeing.
And in that pressure-dark uncoiled
the great desire to escape, to pass the narrow gate
between formlessness and form,
morning sun falling into the room.

He couldn't recall the unremarkable day
when he was taken alive by the machine,
interred in its hallucinations, its noise and grinding dark.
Or the days that followed,
when he shuffled from piano to desk,
or looked out a third-floor window
at electrical wires criss-crossing the street—
a man already half-changed into something else,
arms outstretched like an insect pinned behind glass.

In three rooms of sunlight, that rattled
when the traffic passed, he built a sibylline world
from empty shells: the soundless
representations of sound, operas
written in coloured crayon, sonatinas and *lied*—on paper,
removed from life by a single degree.

It was there I found him,
floating toward me, from narrow hall to door,
hands turned back on themselves like scorpions
or the arched spines of dancers—
his expression pale, astonished
as a drowned man rising in a lake.
And in his tangled hair,
music.

You will never be whole, he told me,
that is your beauty
and the mystery of how everything begins again,
but in silence *(... comment tout recommence,*
mais en silence.)

This morning an email arrived from Paris.
In the Hospital Pitié-Salpêtrière a man's body uncurls
for the first time in 70 years.
Chère Judith, it begins,
Je suis désolé ...

In the distance I hear an aeroplane coming.
He will lean into an oval window,
to watch archipelagos of townlights unfold over black—
a highway of luminous points builds itself
straight out over nothingness.
And he will name it *la porte étroite*,
the narrow gate.

Dinner Party at Ness

A rotting beach house at day's last watch.
Figures edge an oval table,
winebottles, tumblers repurposed
from vegemite jars.
At arm's reach, an oyster bucket teeters
on a piano stool—the piano itself silent,
a monolith, more sideboard than instrument,
its closed lid, a shelf for buoys
and the found skulls of birds.

I stay past the floor lamp's reach.
A drunk girl arranges herself on a chaise,
watching the lit half of the room—
where a costume designer flirts
with a septuagenarian,
her boyfriend staring into a half-drained glass
of cheap but palatable wine.

The drunk girl rolls her eyes
at a theatre director in a MOMA T-shirt.
He holds the floor,
rolling out anecdotes like a machine—
arguments won, famous people
he once had dinner with;
he speaks like a machine,
like someone afraid of the unspeakable.
While outside, the coast settles
to cicada and still,
the passing thud of wallabies.

Called out by branches, the drunk girl
wraps her shoulders in a crocheted rug
and slips away—
through sliding doors,
the verandahs of unmended chairs, now tattered,
now faded by salt,
and I follow.

Under broad front stairs, she shows me a gull
headless, half-buried by leaves.
The answer is always like that:
kabbalah, peyote, the tarot—no matter how we ask,
the answer comes only in images
we already know.

Tonight the stars are closer,
last light vivifies the bark,
ignites a brown dam silver.
I feel it like inhaling the sun,
the whole nocturnal coast surging to life.

Inside, the theatre production is in full swing.
The drunk girl starts to snore.

I escape, where air cools
but does not rob heat from the dirt.
Orion vanishes in a movement of leaves.
Down the snarled track,
past dogbait signs to the clearing,
silence amplifies a snapping twig,
a frogmouth slices air—and something watches,
something shifts in the scrub.

My hand on a snowgum's paper skin
leaves a shadow—wormlines,
brown over chalk;
a connection of woman and tree
in the last seconds before dark.

The reserve thins to shell lines,
a shape graces the edge of water—white
and ocean lit.
I bend down to stare into the glazed eye
of a shark, air-drowned and crippled,
Already dogs have savaged half its side.

This transformation,
this dissolve of bone, breath and gesture—
this is the last music I will write.

Woodstock

Untended is the garden
near Randwick racecourse,
where once God walked with Adam—but forgot him.
And oyster was the Eden of his forgetting:
where Billy Graham preached to fifty thousand,
his praises lifting above that sea of hallelujahs,
the roar of Kings Cross evangelists
pulling up on Harleys.

In the 70s my father was a Pentecostal flame,
walking the 3am streets like Dylan,
steel-string on his back
before tides of Hyde Park untouchables,
the drunks and Darlinghurst prostitutes,
rolled in for soup and a lift to the red cross.
They found Christ at our breakfast table each morning
and lost him again by noon.

At bedtime, my brother and I, quiet
as a pepper tree traces patterns in a doorway's light,
the downstairs drift of Joni Mitchell singing
stardust caught in the Devil's bargain
(*and we gotta get back to the garden.*)

Our father, leaning in the hall,
unwound stories of missionaries
smuggling bibles into the Middle East—
and how faith kept the bullets from their flesh,
and how faith planted tiny mustard seeds
in the marrow of their spines

that decade by decade, grew into flowering offshoots
of the one sacred plant.

In the late hours, our mother strummed into a silent house
her guitar strings reaching out in vastness,
like Stockhausen building spaceships out of sound.
She was so tired of waiting for Jesus
after all that investment, the deprivations and prayer,
faith like a shrinking line,
hard to hold, it cuts the palm.

But the transvestite with dyed hair wasn't Christ,
though he came with wounds in his hands,
quickened with holy rage and quickened
with the psilocybin fragments of Our Lord.

If we'd praised more, if we'd believed
till tongues of flames descended to our heads,
perhaps we'd have erased the image
of my sister's infant coffin, painted white
and painted in the garage when family budgets
did not extend to funeral costs,
our green Valiant, unregistered and up on blocks,
an ambulance struggling in traffic.

Our father borrowed money for a suit—
all of Eden hidden inside his briefcase,
brass latches snapped down to keep it safe
through days of trains and black umbrellas,
the senseless ambulations of a body
no longer guided by anything inner.

But decade by decade,
the mustard seed moving,
the plant rising sacred in his limbs.
He speaks a garden
and the garden comes into being,
where pine needles whisper at his feet
and know him from the sassafras and musk,
from the the serpentine coils of his DNA.

Unsummonable are the dead.
She will not come again to the shade of his mandarin trees,
toy rabbit cradled inside her coat,
or lain down in autumn drifts,
her body covered with leaves,
as dead leaves pile upon dead leaves.
Where sadness gives the crows glossolalia,
they open their throats
and the whole stellar vault rushes out of their bodies.

In the end, it is only night that returns to the garden
where once God abandoned Adam
to the dark opium, to wormwood.
and numbing sleep,
and everything was finally folded in sleep.

Mythopoeia

She, from bare garden, steps
through a hedge, past the suburb's last house—
playing fields made enormous by night
to the blind lawn edge,
where treelines

inhale the dark. The glittering stones,
silent stormdrains, sky—
the stars silent.

And if a red hare were to slide
from ancient grass,
a sly and ancient light would come
if she wished it.

And she wished

to be a whole animal
not this chimera, fog-bodied
and written in the dark
and written into the wandering ring
where late hours press against her body.

The red hare
stands up inside a man,
ti-tree and fire step him out—
breathes through him a magic, night-formed and strong
and he tells her: *Kandanga daruarungu manangga gilbanga*
star falling at night,
go back.

Windlines
through seething tussock are moving in
and it is midnight,
it is midnight over everyone we have loved.

She was with you there, *mirntiwarri*,
with you the whole time,
but you were not with her.

Sommernachtstraum

—for Irene Lamprecht

I love you
from a fear of loneliness,
said the Minotaur.
Perhaps he'd not spoken,
but she'd known it
from the restless sound of his bellowing
deep in the ornamental garden.

She sees him grown tiny with distance;
a figure with weighted head,
disappearing into an erotica of trees.

And for the longest time
they circled near to one another.
She, in the avenues of burned Lindens,
the shadows cast by cold war television antennas;
and he, in the *Dämmerung*,
the mythical spaces of Goethe and Heine,
touching reality only as something profane:
the imp perched on a sleeper's chest
or a half-transparent figure seen in fog
by early morning cyclists.

She keeps a photograph of him
taken in his studio
he is painting nature morte,
halved fruit in an antiquated style,
but she liked how light fell across his hand
and how his body and hers were separated only

by paintbrushes in a jar
and cigarette smoke.

The picture frame breaks and is never mended.
She fills her apartment with orchids
and recordings of Peking opera;
but in the nights,
near Teufelsberg, where there are no Minotaurs
and lichen falls like old woman's hair,
she lies between hulls of abandoned cars
searching for satellites.

II. The stag wears a man's skin.
Birds scatter on the hunter's path.

Night of the Fish

Near Wycliffe Well,
roadside stalls sell gasmasks and binoculars.
Travellers stop here for T-shirts with pictures of aliens
in cowboy hats or slogans like "The Truth is Out There."

After Vietnam they came in Kombi vans
to plant orchards, or just outrun the gunfire in their heads.
Drove all night—the highways of roadkill,
into dust and burnt-umber
mirages of Jesus on the tar.

In the 1980s,
three trackers in a dodge charger
were chased along the pass from Tennant Creek
to the Devil's Marbles by UFOs.

They recalled the play of stroboscopic lights
over monoliths that, in nightheat, seemed to evanesce
and how waterholes resembled the mouths of bass.

Wycliffe Well Petrol Station & Van-park
was renovated for tourist crowds that never came.

In the bar, truck drivers had photographs taken
with inflatable aliens
or models of the ET dissections at Roswell.

When summer threw its chimeras on the road,
they stayed whole afternoons,
watching satellite TV in their underwear and boots.

And every local has a story
about a comet that set fire to the chookshed,
or the shrill electrostatic sound
that vibrates in the banana fields
when all the tractors have gone.

Did you ever in half-sleep...
In the wide leaves' windless sway...
or when, past bedtime,
missing children were found sleeping
in circles of unnaturally flattened cane...

Come the cool,
this stretch of highway will be lined with the 4x4s
of shamans and contactees.
Phones charged from cigarette lighters,
they'll wait for night, for the glittering UFOs to appear
high against the rock, for the secret,

                              to taste it,
for cirrostratus clouds to flex above the tundra
and restore to them everything lost.

Eyes trained on the ridge,
they won't notice grass snakes rippling without wind,
or wallabies disembowelled beside creeks,
in which are reflected sparks
                    that are not stars—
or how Aborigines walking home
in full midday heat, avoid the shade.

From this place in the middle of the night,
you can look in any direction and see the whole horizon
streaming out, the wolf star,

                                        Vega,
the breathless advance of satellites
and the milky way unfolds its emu
of black spaces.

From the Kombi roof
we watch the landscape, van lights
straggling through rags of trees.
Last sun dips over concrete spaceships,
the statue of Elvis by the gate.

And nothing in this humidity moves.
Park lights
sputter and fail.
The hum of air-conditioners cooling an empty bar.

Banana leaves, outlined silver, sway
like camels walking out,

                        lifting off,
becoming star ships.
They lean into wind,
but there is

                 no wind.
and we can't be sure that we see them,
those sleek grey figures walking out of
no wind.

On the van-park lawn
something spins the plastic flamingos,
French doors on the patio

                                bang.

Tell me.

Have you ever, in half-sleep, seen them?

Only the dogs know for sure.
They go out of their minds,
every dog from here to Tennant Creek,
barking,
facing north.

In the carpark a ute is on fire.

No trace, no trace of anything alive.
Its alarm squeals and dies,
its residue buzzing in the ears.

And we, in stardark, disguise our thoughts
in sound loops of popular songs:
> *Shake up the picture, the lizard mixture . . .*

Someone is always listening to the radio,
somewhere else.
Someone coughs.
Someone closes a door.

In threes, they come circling
through the musculature of dark,
testing bungalow windows and doors—
their shadows lattice the bodies of sleepers
and night tries to climb inside them
without showing its face.

We watch them sweep the van-park,
swivelling like the necks of peacocks,
the fruit tree pythons who, while we sleep,

swallow kittens in the yard.

At Wycliffe Well,
while the petrol station plays Duran Duran songs
to empty bowsers,
they come wandering slowly toward us
across the highway.

In Krakow

Before the thousand-eyed cathedral,
a homeless man sinks to his knees
wreathed by gliding breasts of pigeons.
He is singing almost without sound
                    Panis Angelicus.
Light fails and the birds,
air lifting through their feathers like breath,
in vain use their silence to reach him.

Letter to Marilyn

You died eight days ago
and I have taken your children
to the beach house at Ness,
where tide pool rocks assume the form
of an antlered stag.

I photograph Grace on her surfboard,
Grace in diamond water
closing over her head like a mouth.
It gathers her up in blueness
and when she rests gangly arms on the tide,
you are the rusalka swimming beneath her;
that in her blood vessels, swims.

Landscape returns to a house.
We arrange pipefish, a Mexican flower,
the skull of a bird—a nature morte scavenged
from glass-fronted cabinets.
And I see you again in motelight,
in the tilt of Beni's face, as he tells me:
when I die, I'll find her again
in the world's belly.

Marie-Luis watches eucalypts drop kingfishers
into the merciless lake.
She is mute,
she hides her mouth behind her hand,
and at night, she paints me a picture of dawn—
the stag, looking in through curtains,
sun rolling between his antlers.

Wolf Hunt

—for Victoria Royds

Those cosmonauts who looked for God in outer space
but did not find him, returned to soviet ice
and the hunting of wolves.

      Do you remember?
      On the tenth night of Marilyn's death,
      we are standing in a Canberra backyard
      reciting books of the dead.

      And we know she will come,
      lured by sound and cold on the tongue that names her—
      moving from window to window
      to the first floor room where her children sleep.
      And pressing her hand to the glass,
      sadness will enter the bedroom like a sea,
      outstretched, withdrawn as she goes.

      To this backyard of shale and tempest
      only cold remains,
      where winter leaves interrogate
      the walls of a house
      and we are reciting Tibetan verses
      to lift her up in praise,
      to lift her up as ash praising,
      as white moths turning,
      as soft hair escaping from a braid.

On the ice-covered tundra,
men run in heavy sheepskin.
A wolf is shot, tumbles in a brume of snow.

Die Wilde Jagd

These dog-days,
heavy with the incubation of storms,
we drag folding chairs
to the edge of a carpark;
concrete-edged garden
facing an expanse of weeds and plastic bags
waiting for wind.

You open an art journal from Berlin—
paintings from folktales: the Erl-King and Wild Hunt
"too romantic", you say.

But I have seen them sleeping in the fields—
albino animals: horned and harelipped,
carnal as plants;
their bodies undressed by flies
and the heat that flattens.
They signal to each other
with the clicking tongues of bones under grass.

The Berlin Philharmonic, who once
performed the Ninth Symphony for Hitler,
this season reclaims Beethoven,
whose portrait hangs over the mantelpieces of Weimar,
six kilometres from Buchenwald.

Clouds racing their own shadows,
evoke miasmas of horsemen, flared nostrils
and severed limbs. Wind, tasting of salt, hums
through cans and shopping trolleys
like a call of flugelhorns
and the dogs are barking.

An essay by Gunter Grass repeats his warning:
that the moving train is programmed for disaster.
Commuters press their faces to the glass,
for a glimpse of Brandenburg Gate,
its warhorses shaken by jackhammers,
by an orchestra playing the Ninth
between bulldozers.

Do you see the antlered man turning
in a machinery of trees,
his hair thick with the resin of oaks?
He turns on us a gaze made desolate by limepits
and the abattoir's musk;
a gaze that utters *an die Freude* like a love poem,
while from his open palms uncoil
the carrion-birds.

I reach for your hand
but you have already gone.

III. She looks for him in the interiors of dead things;
the exuviae of wasps, the dried carcasses of animals.

The Wedgetails

"The sea is not less beautiful in our eyes because we know
that sometimes ships are wrecked by it."
(Simone Weil)

King tide, January 1976.
The beach is an ivory line between spruce.
Aeroplane-armed, my brother runs
through waist-high grass,
sunlight skittering around him,
lifts static in his thin hair.

From open sea, a *kurruwarri* wind,
lungs of the breath that formed us,
that wove us together in secret;
when we were magicians
and read auguries in tongues of sand.
Mud creepers and whelks—
the sea returns its dead into our keeping.

Mum's paisley sleeves billow
as she waves us in,
the sky flexing, clouds dilate
to anvils above our tent,
and I remember how the sea withdrew.

Through our Valiant's rear window
treelines thin to spinifex,
the ochre bulls of dust rise,
shoulder to shoulder, where we pass.
In the microsecond before dark
a wedgetail spirals to light
between gigantic clouds.

It is night. The radio emergency channel
mutters under ululating gales.
My brother sits between front seats
his face tinted green by the dash,
crossed by fishtailing windscreen wipers.
And in the south-west, ant-trails of semi-trailers
wind away and vanish.

Our breath pools opal on the windows.
We watch for shapeshifters:
ochre-striped and dark at the breast—
holes where the rain does not fall,
(*mirlalypa*) we watch for holes in the rain.

To this sanctum of wind and silence and wind
we arrive endlessly,
always following road trains,
snaking endlessly into cyclone—
where omen-clouds advance like icebreakers,
and into the last slivers of light
the wedgetails come folding in.

Sehnsucht

I stand with you again
on the platform
at Gesundbrunnen station.
Bright hive of factories,
naked fingers of trees,
pigeons huddle
in the domed truss—and I,
wrapped somnolent,
in your coffee-scented arm, turn
to watch an unremarkable
4 o'clock moon
a not-quite half-moon;
as clouds drift over it
like veils
on a woman's breath.
Suddenly I am very awake,
a living witness
to this unrepeatable moment:
cloud evanescing
from ordinary moon.
And the train comes—
a plump lady hangs
in the aisle,
her Indian earrings sway
as the carriage moves.
She catches my eye,
her smile: the sun.
And I am already back
in my apartment,
last station

unseen,
walk home
forgotten,
stairs,
key in the door,
lost.
Only this soliloquy
of cloud passing, stranger smiling,
everything else eaten
by the moon.

I am Freyja

I am Freyja of the ice fields,
following a narwhal's tusk
through diamond-threaded air—
for he has retracted speech into his jawbone.
And if in sleep, he grazes my naked hip
he will not wake me.
In all the rooms of our house,
snow is falling.

I am Freyja of suburbia,
watching a hills-hoist rotate its shadow
into a caribou's shape,
its velvet nostrils lifting in wind.
And dusk is a cinder path between rooves,
the min-min of headlights on the Parkway,
where a hooded woman walks her dog
in the last light leaving.

I am Freyja, with the driver's door left open,
running back to a rabbit on the road.
Its body unmarked,
one eye turned upward to the moon,
Vega, Europa,
the immense indifference of space.
And he is waiting in the car like a stranger,
streetlights flooding the windscreen,
and we have already begun
not to belong to each other.

I am Frejya
whatever happens now won't matter.
in the cafe of our Fimbulvetr
he will buy me an espresso
and tell me it's over.

Gamma

Nights of winter,
of cloud,
mauve-grey and thin.
Mangroves drop
in the frost-formed creek,
water climbing in darkness.
A white dog
crosses the clearing—
stops, startled by apparitions.
He rotates an ear
in that enormous stellar bowl—
and I know this place,
this stone-lit track
and snarl of sloping trees.
My brother,
sleep has stolen from us this landscape
this sky wandered by satellites
and moist, heavy winds.
A raven spits on a hip of road,
its disembowelled fox thrown from reach
by passing lorries.
And I knew you then, my brother.
I knew your stillness
and did not flinch
at the crash of midnight birds.
In fog, in scarce Pleiades light,
I tasted salt on your mouth
and in your beard,
the dawn.

Sonnenwende

The minotaur, grown old
slumps in an armchair with his back to a lake,
his belly rounded by wine,
by the excess of his peregrinations.
Canvases drape over branches,
drying in sun.

He paints clouds as exotic landscapes: Sumer and Shangri-La,
the colour of the lake at different times of day.
And from memory: he paints the Magdelene,
in flower for the last time,
she who, but for stillbirths, might
have become a pianist.

In portraits, her fingers gesture at the throat,
white, with the poise of long-necked birds.
She is the mater dolorosa of piled up dishes,
of flowers standing dead in a vase.

(She will not forgive him) the wound of laundromats,
the *Ausländerbehörden*;
when they, sliding through the Tiergarten by night,
were lions.

He paints quiet algorithms of exile and return:
the Magdalene transfigured in her Berlin apartment,
when fireworks return the sound of bombings
and pigeons flood her spires.

She is always becoming a painted icon,
a taxidermist's glass-eyed bird.
How late she is restored to him—
this mortis of dust and embalming oil, dragged lifeless
from a museum's vault.

He paints with violence,
every stroke of the brush: a clawstroke
a snapping of the teeth, a strike or blow,
as if to carve his rage into her skin
or cross, by force alone, paint's threshold
to gouge his name
across her water-stained walls.

IV. It is late.
Covering the mirror with a dropsheet,
she calls the dead.

Light Picture

—for Marilyn Meier

In your last photograph, you are standing in front of the house
in a t-shirt dress and thick glasses.
Your scalp is visible through tufts of hair.
At your throat, a pendant blurs in movement,
a spark passing—like the conscious flash an instant before sleep.

Behind you, the dog waits by a waterbowl,
her kennel half-hidden by plants
and I remember gang-gangs turning grey circles
above a wire-fenced yard where two women face each other,
a camera between them.

What struck us most was the sound of the shutter.
Light, bouncing back from your body, imprints itself on film
before reaching my eye. Light binding us together—you and me,
the lens, camera, dog—in perpetual stillness.

Where this was taken, in the front yard you no longer inhabit,
you seem more real because we were there together.
And I can believe you have not died, but only vanished
behind the roses you refused to prune
or down the dirt-packed drive.

You smiled for me, for the camera, as though it cost nothing
and I pressed the shutter too early, caught you mid-turn:
an event-horizon of motion and nonmotion coexisting
at the limits of available light.

This photograph reassures me you were real,
you were seen by me, left fastened in the present,
while you are moving backwards, away from me in time.
It straddles two universes: in one you are alive
and in the other, you are not.

But no light recorded the photograph's immediate future
or past: you told me the cancer had mutated—dustmotes
settling on chairs and doors, the scattered clothes, walls.
You insisted we go outside into sun.

And I remember the sprinkler shuddering across the lawn,
my headlights reversing, lighting up wet grass.

De Profundis

By the fiberglass statue of Aphrodite
at the swimming-pool's edge,
she watches the invisible children
appear and disappear,
their shapes echoed by silhouetted palms
in the hotel windows,
the arabesque of flies over garbage cans.
In Chinese restaurants
their voices wind through vases of cut flowers,
the steam coiling on a teacup's lip.
On pedestrian crossings, they wheel about her
like a bitter wind, rearranging dead leaves
to forms in the air
and later, in the television's blue light,
her elbows jutting against glass
she watches the rain sweep sideways;
only she and the neon of late night supermarkets,
she and the rain-black road,
the slight weight of an empty hand.

Satellite

A winter without snow.
Spectral light transforms an empty railway platform.

From the windbreak of vending machines,
I watch her move through a debris of Roma caravans;
      a man's coat, crystal brooch,
      a face made fragile by the rain.

She stops to smile at a boy, waving
from a playground rocket;
tiny cosmonaut against the mother-ship
of concrete apartment-blocks.

And in the chill of that wide air, she gazes out
at the train-line turning toward Wodzislaw Slaski.
A stray wind strums the telephone wires
and plastic shopping bags float past her head
                      like ash.

As the train comes
I see her place a flower inside a cigarette box.
She is the self hidden from herself
in that cold place.

Liver Cancer

Always the same landscape—
bloated fields.
The wind throws a harrier's scream
across a sanctum of trees.

Fences collapse at the river's icy throat
where dovecotes, empty of doves
emerge like black angels, stepping out
from behind the pines.

We follow troughs in the snow,
past farm machinery and hives
until the monstrous house; night
lowering behind us like an eyelid.

Outside a figure waits on the gravel path
and nothing will keep him out;
not your locked door,
not the slashes of your staircase.

Disguised as birds
he flies darkly at the glass.
Abide with us.

Gargantua

—for Tobias Plebuch

Into that giant northern winter
we walked out
and frost walked beside us,
turning, fold upon fold,
over the black torsos of pines—
smoke,
lifting from the powerplants
weightless and blue.

From the *eintritt verboten*
of a barbed-wire fence we landed knee-deep
in snow purpled by a ferris wheel's shade.
Past swanboats stacked in dry waterslides,
and out, into the cold that deadens—
cold sweeping from the toppled spines
of concrete dinosaurs,
their hulls patterned by wind
and the footprints of birds.

And in that expanse,
where an ice-sheeted canal
extends its emptiness into the North Sea,
we stood and were
wordless.

Der Spiegel

He pauses in the warm air rising
from a U-Barn station
for a cigarette,
or just to see how the citrine light reflects
in icicles under streetsigns;
then walks on,
following the river's curve
into quiet unearthliness, vacuum
without birds or pedestrians, sliding
between cars immured in snow
and the icebound canalboats.

He walks thinner than a soldier's trace
again, through Soviet lines—
Toska of night trees,
where the victory angel hangs
above discarded new year's eve rockets
and bottles trapped in ice.
And ringed by cannons from three Prussian wars,
he sits on cardboard;
office lights, glimmering through pines
and bestiaries of shadow
under their branches.

From their balcony in Kreuzberg,
she watched schoolchildren paint giant cosmonauts
on bricks scarred by machinegun fire.
They cut photographs from prohibited magazines:
splinterbombs and wire, the *Geisterbahnhöfe*
where trains do not slow—

and read fairytales in slavonic languages;
of wild stags that erupt from sleeping men,
while for the sleeper, years pass
in an eyelid's fall

                      augenblick.

He makes rosaries of black ice
rolling each bead between his fingers
until dawn blankets him in snow-light
so perfect that morning red cross workers
hesitate to disturb him; as if,
should they come closer,
even this last light would scatter.

And when they leave,
snow retains the curve of his skull
and ice shears from winterheavy branches
with the bellow of antelopes.

V. He is wolf-infested,
a vessel for doppelgängen.
Sometimes he sounds just like a man speaking.

Hyperborea

—for Philip Salom

On René Daumal's *Mount Analogue*

While the summits of all mountains, real or allegorical
are covered in cloud, their torsos reach down
from opacity to the solid plateau—
always, the doorway to the invisible is visible.

Near Mount Ararat, monks travel in moving chapels:
vessels in a shipless land, and when the fog comes,
even these buildings are lost.

I arrived in sunlight, to Gabriel's face carved
on a chapel door, woodlice swarming across his mouth.
And they showed me where the sun, *Shamash,*
is born each morning between mountain peaks—
but no one could recall the path that led there.

In those brooding days, visions came like a heated wind.
I watched a Caspian stag drag its tines through branches,
jet shadow, now light—and Ararat,
rising weird above the cedars.

(In faerie stories, you can't reach the summit
just by following a deer)

On the high mountain face, under ice
that has not melted in human memory,
live the doppelgängen,
their bodies are hollow, like pockets of trapped air,
silver-grey—but sunlight makes them blue.

They only eat carrion, goats fallen to crevices
or migration-exhausted birds—
anything they can drag under ice.
The doppelgängen can't come out into the air
but they can rise to the surface, looking for a door.

They are afraid of light.
They look for a door.

When the stag waded toward the mountain,
I followed, waist-deep in steppe grass
and the wild herbs used for Kurdish tea,
until ridges, like the backbones of giant fish,
grew from bare, clanking rock
and lichens lay breathless under snow,
wide drifts into which I sank, and always
the stag waiting at the limits of sight.

When you set foot on the mountain,
your doppelgänger feels it, as a guitar string feels
the vibration of a neighbouring string.
It knows how to wait, camouflaged
in verglas layers of rock,
in the lighter and darker bands of snow.

At night I sleep on carpets wedged between stones,
so as not to accidentally roll out onto the ice.
In the far valley, monastery lights appear
one by one.

(In faerie stories, there is only one way
to reach the summit)

When your doppelgänger comes to the surface,
you must grab it firmly—
give it no time to react.
Dive into its body, laying your spine along its spine,
wriggling your arms and legs into place.
Then pull your combined limbs out into the air— slowly,
leaving the torso below.

Now you are two beings in one body:
mountaineer and doppelgänger,
limbs sticking out of the ice like a spider.

Now the mountain, real and metaphorical,
will recognise you and lower its defences.
Now we are in the mountain and it is in us.
We have come to understand the sun with our bodies.

The doppelgänger's eyes open inside my lids—
its iris is mine, our pupils narrow and dilate
in exact concurrence.

With doubled sight,
the summit looks like a swarm of moths.
Unbroken snow makes miracles of anything not-snow—
feathers from a nondescript bird, a wind-travelled leaf.
To ice, the difference between dead and living things
doesn't really matter.

Down the fall line, the world is in mid-creation—
new mountains slip from the vaginas of glaciers,
thaw carves channels for unborn rivers.

And on Ararat's peak, light incarnates in everything,
resounding between ice and ice-cloud, light manifests
luciforme a luce prima, light formed from first light.

The Caspian stag tilts his antlers and roars,
microcosm of the mountain, who once screamed out
volcanic ash into the Araxes river.

Plane by plane, the stag vanishes in fog—
legs first, then his torso,
curved antlers stay a moment longer,
suspended in feather-grey,
like an Amen.

Thus Spake the Wolf

You had a vision but told no one:
that the world healed would not be the world restored,
but something new—wilder, and yet the same.

A city lake,
darkness, unillumed by candleflame birches,
the reflected symmetries of lit museums—
we walk where fog does not erase us
and inside you paces a wolf who wants to be a man.

In the night's firm, how silent the trees,
how soft is the whirring of possums.

And tomorrow you will tell me:
'Obviously,
I'm going to walk away from this.'
un peu, beaucoup, passionément,
â la folie, pas du tout …

We return to places that don't exist,
the mystery that leaves hoof-prints in the yard
and strips branches from avenues of lindens.
Each morning the scratch-marks seem more bestial.

I am afraid to feel this: my body lying under yours,
or the swift turning light that enters your window.
I try to draw your body's shape on the wall,
but the shadows won't stop shifting—
a shoulder, now a hip or thigh,
the form veers away.

And this changing of bodies into light
will become only melancholia.
By morning, the light will blind us
and seem darker than the darkness.

When you sleep, the wolf wakes inside your skin.
He says: I am the war,
the one who conceals in your hair
woods and rivers of a forgotten place.

Today you text me from Harlem,
words from a fortune cookie,
something about books and minds—and I imagine you
sliding through the streets like a ship or cloud,
and in front of a Chinese restaurant
people run to escape the rain.

You appear to me like a half-demolished building—
An apartment, cut in half, sways above a rubble courtyard.
The dining table is set and photographs sit on the sideboard.
The slightest breeze could sweep it all away.

Over a faux Han-Dynasty roof,
a new sun rises like a hagfish.

And light will come again into the darkness,
but darkness will not understand it.

Clair de Lune

—for Alan Gould, who knows the sea

When she wakes,
she wakes in the salt of breakers,
in mist that occludes and reveals night's lustre:
the great nocturnal winds
on which arctic terns bear themselves
and are reflected, silver needles
on a black-glass sea.

Through shallows where gulls careen away
and rocks are seen only when the surf retreats,
she is carried out like an embryo,
into the amniotic ocean, thundering to itself
all through the humid night.

And she who swims out will not return.
Another will emerge in her place,
shaking off water.

She won't remember walking toward the sea's green wall,
her unbuckled sandals left on the dunes,
or how she grew lonely among the screens,
liquid crystal inhabitants of a country
where nothing breathes.

Once, in Sunday school, they told her
God made angels from eternity itself,
that they exist not in time, but of time,
trapped in the spaces between the temporal
and the Absolute.

Lost astronauts, unaware of the interstellar cold
in which they hang, their feathers rippled by solar winds,
a psalm heard only by their own kind:

Wandering stars, for whom it is reserved ...

They detach from kelp's shadow, waiting
for the hand of the wave to pass
and in its crash, uncoil.

She sees them levitating on the crests—
a brilliance, immense and old,
leaning out into the prow of night,
spray ionising in their hair,
and the light from shoreside tourist hotels,
razoring through their arms.

They collect in eddies,
where cobalt lies close to the horizon,
light paths
indistinguishable from the trace of time-lapsed stars—
light that has trekked billions of years,
across nebulae and novas, bears rimmed with frost
and the chairs of Cassiopeia.

She floats with her back to the shore
and knows herself
as a time-binding animal.
The fusion of past-stars and future-sea
takes place now in a simple flick of her iris.

Der Doppelgänger

After the flashlights
had returned from the escarpment
and the reproach of neighbours gave way
to a silence more brutal,
she would tell them of the black trees,
the white trees;
rooted grave, where the sun has no access.
And the dog glimpsed
between elbows of thick branches:
a dog who owned no shadow
or whose shadow assumed the shape of birds
and who carried a child's shoe in its mouth
through woods that no real dog would enter;
woods ringed by autobahns and grown
on the rubble of destroyed apartment blocks
and soviet tanks.
And where it passed, she wrapped wire
around the trunks of the pines:

      stark

        white

          stark.

In another room
the television drones a test pattern.
But now she stands in an open window
as wind moves across the yard
and folds her floral curtains
into her arms.

VI. For a short time, two rivers run side by side. One vanishes underground, the other merges into the sea. Once caught in a current, the task of jumping from one river to another is not at all straight-forward.

The Myrrh-bearers

—for Benjamin John Eagleton

The day I truly understood that we are alone
and that love is nothing
but the resounding of my own voice
in the lacunae of my skull,
I was caught in Sydney traffic.

And I knew he would not wait,
this uncle, who had hidden death inside him for so long,
it had become *poïesis*,
the secret fire, in whose light
all transitory things are unspeakably beautiful.

Clouds, now and then,
graze the hospital roof as I, two hours late,
arrive, park the car,
run.

I found him in a turquoise room,
the blood uncirculating,
his face marked with stitches from failed operations.
And I remember a blade of light opened against the wall
as I entered and vanished as the curtains fell closed.

Yea, though we pass through the shadow,
I and the myrrh-bearers
who recited *Our Father, who art ...*
but could not finish,
who faltered and stood voiceless
in the awkwardness of prayer,

my Aunt's fingers unlacing from his—
a small letting go.

At Rookwood, currawongs migrate back
into salt and ether, folding into cloud,
folding back into His tiny mustard seed.

For theirs is the Kingdom.

To this dug-up clay,
to insects and snails,
the desperate resistance of roots,
we commit his body.

Lion Sun, the Holy Sun
comes down to ignite the pines,
if we'd stopped him smoking,
if he'd lived another ten minutes,
if I'd driven faster—
fire consumes us all.

My Aunt, in her red shoes,
drops roses in the mud.
She is the unimaginable seed of catastrophe,
the comet that will hit Russia next week
and carve burning holes in the snow.

To decide to live, despite the hours,
the daily repetition of his absence,
we gather in his garden—
eucalypts, stately in wind.
Sometimes a car passes.

And we tell her,
Rosie, this is what we have saved,
take them, these handfuls of salt,
these photographs.
Here he stands in a lit doorway
or restrings a guitar.

Such a long walk from the garden to the door.
She carries our gifts into the house
and returns with empty arms.

Once as a child, I followed him across a rocky field.
It was night and he moved ahead
through wildflowers and flint—just a shape,
a blackness in the dark
but I knew he existed somewhere out front,
past seeing.

On the M5 a truck has tipped over.
Police direct four lanes into one.
I give way to a blue sedan,
a girl with bobbles in her hair
waves at me through a rear window.

What I wanted to tell him that day,
in just a few sentences,
I am saying it now, poem after poem.
For forty-two days now I have been driving to Sydney
to reach my uncle in time.

Like Honey is the River

Heat, from fire-blackened stones rattles
the cicada-heights:
On these banks I am pigeon-speckled,
in light filtered through a hijab repurposed as sarong.
And every particle contains the whole god divided
in fractions—the pleroma descending
where grey gums share no common shape,
and tumble out their limbs into breathless,
unimaginable blue.

The Shoalhaven River expands rings
about these three children,
floating back to back in lucid shallows,
eddies tugging at their hair
and the river's skin dissolves a floating sun.

In birdlight like this,
I have known chiaroscuros of shade
unfolding greater and lesser abstractions:
frogmouths conjured under bark,
or farm dogs ghosting through tussock.

When her water is mercury;
when dark weighs cloudless on her banks,
the river returns to me these children,
stepping out of reed, fire against their faces
and the great night moving at their backs.

At this urban edge, stellar fields
unroll their microscopia

and a car radio plays *auld lang syne.*
Three children write their mother's name
with the sulphur trails of sparklers—
my friend who loved riverlight
but surrendered her short hours
to Chopin variations.

And I will tell them: her whole kingdom
is spread out over the earth
but we don't see it.

Love Poem

—*for B.W.*

O nobly born, listen undistractedly.
In the Bardo, where all things are like the void and cloudless sky
and the naked, spotless intellect is without circumference or centre.
Know that I am setting you face to face.
(Tibetan Book of the Dead)

At the moment of death
I am watching tamarind trees shudder in the yard.
Something conceals itself past the shade-banded fence.
Sunlight, growing brighter, pours through trellises and vines,
enraging the retina
and you are walking toward me,
disappearing in the excess of light.

Listen undistractedly

At the moment of death
I am crossing a dark harbour toward Tokyo;
my body combed out like wires,
half-luminous in the cool sway of kelp
and lights reverberating from tankers.

Where all things are void and cloudless

I am thirst, craving,
the inquietude of muttonbirds,
lured out too far when the wind drops,
magnetic lines lost in the susurrus and swell.

Without circumference or centre

And remembered in a sound:
your voice reciting books of the dead,
your voice wading through seaweed and foam
unravelling everything.

At the moment of death
I am hanging pendulous as fruit
over a white metal bed,
watching my body dressed by mourners.
And you are arranging stuffed animals
and flowers on a trolley.

I am setting you face to face

You do not see the spider of my nudity
in the angle between ceiling and wall.

And I want to tell you something
about love or forgetting
but all my tongues are scattered
and dazzling.

Acknowledgments

Thanks goes to those kind souls who braved winter evenings in Berlin, Krakow and Canberra reading multiple drafts of this collection. I am especially grateful to Gary Nihsen, Paul Hetherington, Geoff Page, Philip Salom, Anthony Lawrence, Alan Gould, Adam Zagajewski, Greer Versteeg, David Musgrave, Richard Toovey, Melanie Brazzell, Adam Chrambach, Kristin Reynolds, Liane Schneider and Ben Willson.

Poems in this collection are also published in *Axon: Creative Explorations, Journal of the Berlin Creative Writing Group, December Magazine* and *The Ballarat International Foto Biennale Catalogue.*

Poems also appear in the anthologies *The House is Not Quiet and The World is Not Calm: Poetry from Canberra*, edited by Kit Kelen and Geoff Page and *Open Windows: an English-Chinese Anthology of Contemporary Australian Poetry*, edited by Paul Hetherington.